Copyright © 2019 SuperSummary

All rights reserved. No part of this publication may be reproduced, transmitted, or distributed in any form, by electronic or mechanical means, including photocopying, scanning, recording, or file sharing, without prior permission in writing from the publisher, except as provided by United States of America copyright law.

The purpose of this study guide is to provide supplemental educational material. It is not intended as a substitute or replacement of THEIR EYES WERE WATCHING GOD.

Published by SuperSummary, www.supersummary.com

ISBN – 9781712644508

For more information or to learn about our complete library of study guides, please visit http://www.supersummary.com

Please submit any comments, corrections, or questions to:
http://www.supersummary.com/support/

TABLE OF CONTENTS

Their Eyes Were Watching God is the second novel of Zora Neale Hurston, a writer and anthropologist associated with the Harlem Renaissance. Originally published in 1937 by J.B. Lippincott, the book is regarded as one of the forerunner texts of 20th-century African-American and American women's literature. Set in Central and South Florida, the novel is the story of Janie Crawford's evolution from impressionable, idealistic girl to self-confident woman.

Plot Summary

The novel opens with a frame narrative. Janie Crawford, the widow of Joe "Jody" Starks, the former mayor of Eatonville, comes home after disappearing with a younger man she married shortly after the death of her husband. Janie is shabbily dressed, so the townspeople assume the young man took all her money and abandoned her. Eager to understand the truth and to help out her friend, Pheoby Watson visits Janie, who not only tells Pheoby about what happened while Janie was away but also fills in details about her life before Eatonville.

When Janie was 16 and becoming aware of love and sexual desire, she made the mistake of kissing a boy who was walking down the road in front of her house. Nanny Crawford, the grandmother who raised her since birth, forced Janie to marry Logan Killicks, a prosperous but crude farmer who disappointed Janie when it came to love.

Intent on discovering something beyond Logan's farm, Janie fell in love with Joe, whom she encountered on the road as he headed to the all-black town of Eatonville. Joe seduced Janie with the ambitious promises about the impact the two of them would have in this town, but she found the town as stifling as Joe's control of her self-expression.

Joe died of kidney failure when Janie was in her 40s, leaving her independently wealthy. Rather than bowing to pressure to marry another man like Joe, Janie began a romance with Vergible "Tea Cake" Woods, a handsome, adventurous, yet poor man many years her junior. Janie scandalized the town by dating and then marrying him. The couple left Eatonville and, after a brief interlude in Jacksonville that forced Janie to accept Tea Cake as the freewheeling man he was, they moved to the Everglades, where they worked as seasonal migrants and became the center of the rough society there.

Their mostly idyllic time in the Everglades came to an end when a hurricane destroyed Southern Florida. During their flight away from the storm, Tea Cake contracted rabies. Tea Cake, maddened by untreated rabies, attempted to shoot Janie, who killed him in self-defense. Janie was tried for his murder and acquitted.

After hearing Janie's story, Pheoby expresses her own desire to have more adventures and to expand her vision of what a woman can be. Once captive to Nanny's vision of marriage and respectability, by the end of the novel, Janie has embraced the natural vision of love she first saw under the pear tree—and finds herself in the process.

Chapters 1-4

Chapter 1 Summary

The gossips who sit on the porch of the general store in the all-black town of Eatonville, Florida, are curious when Janie Starks, the widow of the former mayor, returns from a mysterious trip. In a well-remembered scandal, Janie had left with a much younger man, Tea Cake, after her husband's death. The men observe how beautiful she still is, while the women seem envious and a little glad that to see her shabbily dressed.

Impatient with this talk, Janie's best friend, Pheoby Watson, decides to bring Janie a meal and find out where she has been. Janie tells Pheoby that she married Tea Cake, who has since died. Shocked, Pheoby encourages Janie to end the scandal around the relationship with Tea Cake by telling the town about the marriage; the current gossip is that Tea Cake took all of Janie's money and then left Janie for a younger woman. Janie tells Pheoby that she doesn't care what the town thinks: Janie has seen the world and she still has her money. It turns out that Janie spent her time away in the Everglades, and she decides to tell Pheoby her story. If anyone wants to know the truth of what happened, she says, they can ask Pheoby.

Chapter 2 Summary

Janie was raised by her grandmother, called "Nanny," on the plantation of the Washburns, an affluent white family in West Florida. She ran around the grounds with both African-American children and the family's white children. Janie didn't even know she was black until she saw her darker face in a photo of all the children. Jealous of the clothes and attention lavished on Janie by Mrs. Washburn, the African-American children in this group used to bully Janie about her origins: Janie's father was hunted with bloodhounds presumably after raping Janie's mother, Leafy. Nanny removed Janie from this bullying by buying a plot of land and a house.

Janie feels "her conscious life commenced at Nanny's gate" one afternoon after she watched the bees come and go to the blossoming pear tree in her backyard (10). She was 16 years old, and watching life perpetuate itself in the natural world aroused her innate sexual desire:

> She saw a dust-bearing bee sink into the sanctum of a bloom; the thousand sister-calyxes arch to meet the love embrace and the ecstatic shiver of the tree from root to tiniest branch (11).

When she saw Johnny Taylor, a boy she'd previously considered inconsequential, she sneaked out the gate of her yard to kiss him. Nanny, ever protective of her granddaughter, caught them kissing and angrily called Janie back into the house. This, observes Janie, "was the end of her childhood" (13).

Nanny gave Janie a stern lecture about the reality of her situation: Nanny was old, and she wanted Janie to marry immediately to secure her future. Nanny suggested Logan Killicks, an old and somewhat uncouth man, as the potential husband for Janie. Janie responded with petulant silence; angered, Nanny slapped Janie but then immediately repented. Nanny told Janie that black women were expected to bear the burdens of everyone else.

Born into slavery on a slave plantation in Savannah, Nanny gave birth to Leafy, whose father was Nanny's master. After the owner left to fight in the Civil War, Nanny ran away when the jealous mistress threatened to whip her to death and sell off Leafy, whose light skin and eyes made her parentage obvious. Fortunately for Nanny, Sherman's army invaded—and saved her and Leafy. She eventually ended up with the Washburns.

Nanny refused to marry because she wanted to avoid the possibility that a man would mistreat her daughter. Nanny wanted Leafy to be a teacher, but her plans for her daughter came crumbling down when Leafy was 17, after the teacher tasked with training Leafy raped her and impregnated her with Janie. Leafy was never mentally sound after the assault, and Nanny, who declared herself old and fragile, said that the thought of some man sexually exploiting Janie would kill Nanny.

Chapter 3 Summary

Janie married Logan Killicks, a prosperous if uncouth man with 60 acres to his name, shortly after this talk with Nanny. She talked herself into the marriage despite her misgivings; she felt no love for Logan. The adults in Janie's life thought it a good match, assuming that married people eventually found a way to love one another, but they felt no particular joy when Janie rode off with Logan on their wedding day.

Confused and disappointed by a lack of love and sexual desire after three months of marriage, Janie sought advice from her grandmother. Janie told Nanny that although Logan provided for all her material wants, he was poorly groomed, unattractive, and unlovable. Nanny warned Janie that a man would only put a woman on a pedestal for long, and she scoffed at Janie's desire for love. Chasing after love and the fulfillment of sexual desire led to the downfall of black women, Nanny argued, because it kept them poor. Janie insisted that she wanted "things sweet wid [her] marriage lak when you sit under and pear tree and think" (24).

Nanny refused to listen any longer, but she felt so worried that she had forced Janie into a loveless marriage that she died a month later. Having finally realized that Logan would never deliver the vision of love she saw under the pear tree, Janie began looking outward again. She waited with expectation by the gate of her house, almost as if she thought the thing she wanted would find her.

Chapter 4 Summary

The honeymoon period between Logan and Janie ended after six months. Logan grew weary of pampering Janie and began to demand that she do work outside of the confines of the house, including plowing in the fields. One day while Logan was away, Janie saw a stylishly dressed man named Joe "Jody" Starks walking down the road. A 30-year-old African-American man, Joe had set out for South Florida to help create an all-black town: Eatonville. His ambitions, plans, and flattery intrigued Janie during the two weeks he passed the time with her.

Attracted to Janie, Joe saw her as someone who could help him become an important man in the new town. He asked her to come with him, and Janie initially hesitated; doing so would violate all the moral standards Nanny had taught her. Logan, meanwhile, became convinced that Janie did not love him. He brought up her illegitimate birth and tried to convince her she was lucky to have him. After one more bitter argument with Logan, Janie decided to take Joe

Starks up on his offer. She left home with nothing but her apron, and Jody took her farther south, where the two married.

Chapters 1-4 Analysis

In these first four chapters, Hurston establishes the novel's cultural context and introduces the novel's central themes: African-American women's experiences and their quests for love.

The initial scene juxtaposes the silent Janie returning to town against the chorus of the "porch," a group of townspeople who pass judgment on Janie for violating their values. The voices of the porch bring forth the conservative values of this sleepy Southern town, while the dialect and the rich idioms reflect the importance of oral culture in the African-American South.

Hurston's portrayal of the porch shows how Janie's choice to date a younger man, marry him, and leave town violated the then-prevalent gender and racial norms for black women. The varied reactions also set up the novel's central conflict: whether Janie would bow to societal expectations for African-American women or pursue her own desires, no matter the consequences.

Hurston uses nested, framed stories to help the reader understand how Janie violated those norms. The outer frame is Janie telling Pheoby her story; within is Nanny's story, essentially a slave narrative about how Nanny survived sexual exploitation by her master and the threat of violence from her mistress. Hurston's inclusion of Nanny's fictional story fills in details about slavery frequently missing from the historical record, since men had written most slave narratives published at the time. The outer frame also contains Leafy's story, which shows how vulnerable African-American women still were to sexual abuse even after the end of slavery. Both stories demonstrate the extraordinary challenges African-American women faced as they navigated difficult economic and racial terrain.

Within the outermost frame, Janie tells Pheoby the story of her quest for self-expression and love, which began beneath the pear tree. By painting Janie's desire in such lyrical terms, through descriptions of the natural world, Hurston portrays Janie's desires—and by extension, those of all African-American women—as completely natural, despite the societal pressure to deny them. African-American women writers of the time often feared that discussing their sensuality would confirm the stereotype that African-American women were, by default, promiscuous. By centering this story around an African-American woman's quest for love, Hurston broke new ground, no mean feat in the early 20th century.

Chapters 5-8

Chapter 5 Summary

Janie and Joe arrived in Eatonville, disappointed to discover the town not at all developed. Joe immediately purchased additional land, built a store, bought the town's first streetlamp, and pushed the townspeople to establish a government—and to elect him mayor.

Joe treated Janie like another of the many possessions that showed his superiority to the other townspeople. Although several men in the town attempted to flirt with her, Janie remained closemouthed and unfriendly. The women of the town envied Janie, in part because she followed Joe's advice to present herself as above them by dressing formally.

As time went on, the townspeople learned that Joe, although arrogant and accustomed to having his way, was also willing to work hard to make his ambitions a reality. They wondered how Janie bore her marriage to a man so set in his ways. They also noted how he regularly berated her in front of customers when she made mistakes in the store. Janie began to feel fearful and lonely, realizing that Joe expected Janie to find complete satisfaction in his successes, just as he did. She grew weary of his constant activity.

Chapter 6 Summary

The front porch of Joe's store became the center of the town and the center of its rich storytelling culture. A whole mythology sprang up around a very thin, overworked mule that belonged to Matt Bonner. The porch gatherers regularly told stories about the mule and teased Matt about the way he mistreated it. Joe bought the mule and put it out to pasture after he overheard Janie fret about how the mule's poor treatment. Impressed by the gesture, she gave a public speech to praise his generosity, but the good feeling evaporated when Joe refused to let Janie attend a mock funeral for the mule.

As the years went by, Janie felt increasingly oppressed by Joe's demands for submission. He forced her to work in the store despite how unsuited she was to the work, and demanded that she cover her long hair with a rag after he realized that her hair mesmerized the men. He also slapped her repeatedly when one of her dinners turned out to be inedible.

Although Joe believed he was doing his duty by her by "building a high chair for her to sit in and overlook the world" (62), Janie wanted to participate in community life on the porch. Joe's insistence on absolute obedience slowly suffocated Janie's idealized notion of what marriage and a husband should be. As the years went by, their marriage, especially the physical side of it, shriveled.

Chapter 7 Summary

At 40 (when Joe was almost 50), Janie was physically present in both the store and in her home, but emotionally absent. Janie considered leaving her loveless marriage at times, but could not imagine where she would go.

Joe, meanwhile, wasted away with an unnamed illness. Conscious of how he had diminished physically, he began to ridicule Janie in front of others about her age. One day when Janie made a mistake while serving a customer, Joe insulted her by calling attention to her "rump hangin' nearly to [her] knees" (78). The people in the store laughed at first but stopped when they realized Joe intended to degrade his wife. For the first time, Janie spoke up, insisting that Joe stop insulting her and revealing publicly that he that he was impotent, which astonished the onlookers. Humiliated by the public insult to his manliness, Joe beat Janie until she left the store.

Chapter 8 Summary

After this public rupture, Joe, who continued to waste away from his illness, moved into a separate bedroom and ceased talking to Janie. He began seeing a root doctor, who convinced him that Janie had cursed him and that Joe would only get better with the root doctor's help. Joe was nearly on his deathbed when Janie ignored his coldness and called a doctor. The doctor explained that Joe had been in kidney failure for two years. He was terminally ill because of his failure to get treatment. Janie shared the news with Joe, who seemed shocked by the truth.

Joe tried to force Janie to leave his sickroom, but she refused. She instead told him the truth about how his insistence that everyone—including Janie—bow in submission to him destroyed any possibility of happiness for her. Janie told him a hard truth: "You got tuh die tuh find out dat you got tuh pacify somebody besides yo'self if you wants any love and any sympathy in dis world" (86-7). When Joe died, Janie looked at herself in the mirror; she saw a woman who was clearly middle-aged but still beautiful. Then, she left the room to put on the appearance of mourning that the townspeople seemed to expect.

Chapters 5-8 Analysis

Hurston continues to develop the theme of Janie's quest for identity and does so in the context of the rich storytelling culture of African Americans of the South. Hurston represents Janie's increasing assertion of control over her own identity through Janie's facility with speech and language.

Janie quickly discovered that her idealized notion of material comfort married to romantic love was no more fulfilled with Joe than it had been with Logan. In exacting detail, Hurston presents a patriarchy, specific to Southern African-American culture, that slowly strips Janie of her autonomy. As he did during their courtship, Joe insisted after marriage that Janie have an identity based only on her connection to him. He and the townspeople considered Janie a trophy wife, just another piece of property to prove that Joe Starks was superior to everyone else.

Joe quickly and publicly crushed Janie's efforts to carve out her own place in the community. He refused to let her wear her hair out—the primary symbol of her femininity in the novel—denigrated her in front of others, and even struck her when she cooked a less-than-perfect meal that failed to meet his gendered expectations.

His most oppressive effort to dominate her was his refusal to allow Janie share her opinions, engage in storytelling, or share gossip on the porch with other members of the community. Other women engaged publicly in talk on the porch, which meant that Joe's refusal to let Janie participate had little to do with the community's gendered norms. When Janie finally asserted herself, she publicly attacked Joe's virility. Her outburst most certainly violated those norms, so the community very quickly turned from empathy to exclusion as Joe's physical decline became more obvious.

Janie realized that she would never earn the community's approval, no matter what she did. Her friendship with Pheoby helped her weather this ostracism. In their final confrontation, Janie took Joe to task for his cruelty. Although this conversation made clear that Janie understood her community's cultural expectations for marriage, she later presented herself as a grieving widow, not yet willing to violate all gendered norms.

Chapters 9-13

Chapter 9 Summary

Janie arranged a lavish funeral for Joe, and important people came from all over South Florida to see him off. Janie publicly presented as the grieving widow dressed in expensive black mourning clothes, but she celebrated on the inside, free of restraints for the first time in her life. As she thought of Nanny's decisions, Janie realized she hated her grandmother for foreclosing the possibilities in her life, and blamed Nanny for choosing material security over happiness for her granddaughter.

After the funeral, Janie carried on with her normal routine of minding the store with the help of Hezekiah, Joe's assistant. Free of Joe, she burned all her head rags, wore her hair uncovered, and occasionally sat on the porch. When suitors began showing up just a month after Joe's death, she fended them off by ignoring them. She told Pheoby that she her love for newfound freedom, not grief, led her to deny these suitors. Pheoby told her to keep that subversive thought to herself.

Chapter 10 Summary

Janie was tending the store all by herself on a slow day when Vergible Woods, who went by the name "Tea Cake," walked in to buy some cigarettes. With most of the town away at a baseball game, Janie agreed to sit with Tea Cake and play a game of checkers; she found him instantly charming. He gently flirted with her, flattered her by calling her smart, and—unlike Joe—saw women as capable beings. He treated Janie like a regular woman rather than someone to be placed upon a pedestal.

When the townspeople began to trickle back into town, Tea Cake socialized easily with them and convinced Janie to allow him to walk her home. She had misgivings about walking home with a stranger, but he gallantly left her at her door.

Chapter 11 Summary

With Tea Cake away for a week, Janie was assailed by doubts. She worried what the townspeople would think of her for dating a much younger man and wondered if Tea Cake were after her money. When he returned, to Janie's relief, she played checkers with him on the porch, much to the pleased surprise of the townspeople. He walked her home, and this time sat on the porch with her. He also took Janie out fishing that night, arousing her long dormant sense of play.

Tea Cake, a blues man, played Janie's piano and moved one step closer by grooming her hair while she slept that night. When Janie asked why he was interested in someone so ordinary, he told her he found her far from ordinary and encouraged her to really look at herself. Tea Cake addressed her objections to a relationship directly; he also noted her fear that he was merely after her money. She dismissed his concern about their financial differences but noted that most people might find their age disparity objectionable. Tea Cake said he didn't care about what other people thought, but he left abruptly after Janie told him he might feel differently once the heat of the moment passed.

In the days that followed, Janie tried to think pragmatically about a relationship with Tea Cake but found that she could not escape her desire for the love she had dreamed about under the pear tree. He showed up at daybreak one morning to plead his love again, but rushed away to go to work; then, he showed up on another morning and kissed Janie fiercely enough to wake her from sleep. She finally accepted that she loved him, but her doubts come back again when he disappeared for four days.

When he returned, he had a car, and he asked her to go to the big social event of the year—the Sunday school picnic—and offered to take her shopping beforehand. She asked him earnestly if he wanted to go and make such a public declaration that they were together. He assured her that he did and that he loved her wholeheartedly.

Chapter 12 Summary

When the love between Tea Cake and Janie became clear after the picnic, the townspeople were shocked that "Mrs. Mayor Starks" would date a man so different from her deceased husband (110). Finally, Sam Watson asked Pheoby to talk to Janie to encourage her to put an end to this unseemly relationship.

Pheoby talked with Janie about all the possible ways it could go wrong, but Janie insisted that she knew what she was doing. She explained to Pheoby that her former separation from people like Tea Cake was Joe's doing. Janie hated being idolized and hardly knew what to do with herself because Joe forced her to stay up on a pedestal that kept her lonely and unhappy. Such a life might have suited Nanny, a former slave, but Janie wanted something else.

Janie told Pheoby that she was interested only in love, and she was willing to violate social norms—think "new thoughts" and "new words"—if doing so would bring her happiness on her own terms. Janie closed the conversation by disclosing a bombshell that she asked Pheoby not to share quite yet: She planned to marry Tea Cake, sell the store, and start over somewhere away from the shadow of Joe Starks.

Chapter 13 Summary

Janie received a letter from Tea Cake: He had a railroad job in Jacksonville and wanted Janie to come right away so they could be married. Once Janie arrived, they spent their honeymoon in a boarding house. A week later, Tea Cake left one morning to get some fish but failed to return for a day and a night. Even worse, Janie discovered that $200 hidden in her dress (on the advice of Pheoby) had gone missing. Janie feared that Tea Cake had made a fool of her. As she waited for him, she recalled the story of Mrs. Tyler, an older woman who lost everything when she married a man in Tampa who stole her money and abandoned her. Mrs. Tyler relied on charity to return home and died soon after.

Tea Cake returned. When Janie asked where he'd been and what happened to her money, he told her a long tale about discovering the money and deciding to go on a spending spree so he could feel like a rich man for a day. He threw a catered party for his railroad coworkers and got his guitar out of the pawn shop to top off his spree. Janie seemed more offended that he didn't bother to get her so she could join in the fun than anything else. He explained to her that he was afraid she would look down on his friends, working-class people who worked on the railroad. She told him she loved him and didn't care about any of that, so the two made up.

Tea Cake also assured her that he would get her money back. The upcoming Saturday would be payday for the railroad workers, and Tea Cake considered himself an excellent gambler. Janie had misgivings, but she accepted his decision because she loved him; he was once again gone all night on Saturday, and he returned with two shallow knife wounds and $320. When she told him that she had $1,200 in the bank, he told her to keep it. They would live only on what he brought in from there on out.

Tea Cake decided that they should head to the Everglades, where work and fun were plentiful. She agreed to go with him: She trusted him at this point and felt a "self-crushing love" that snuffed out her fear that he would abandon her.

Chapters 9-13 Analysis

Janie's life changed substantially in the aftermath of Joe's death; at Joe's funeral, she bade goodbye both to him and to conforming to gendered norms. Over the course of a just a few months, Janie came into her own and pursued love on her terms. Her evolution occurred against the backdrop of strong societal pressure to remain chaste, marry within her social class, and allow others—the community and respectable men who supposedly had her best interests at heart—a say in how she lived her life. The love story that unfolds in these middle chapters is subversive when read in historical context.

Janie's identity as a woman changed both outwardly and inwardly. Her most public external declaration of her autonomy came when she burned the head rags Joe made her wear and left her hair uncovered at the store. Janie allowed Tea Cake to touch her hair once she had welcomed him into her home, and she began styling her hair as her courtship with Tea Cake blossomed. Her self-care in this instance reflects the importance of hair culture, especially in the African-American community. Refusing to bow to pressure from the town, Janie exchanged widow's black for color—blue in this case—to publicly acknowledge her relationship with Tea Cake. Her understanding of the risk is expressed in many ways, including the cautionary tale of

Mrs. Tyler, who returned home with dye running from her hair after being conned by Who Flung.

Janie's most significant shifts are internal. As Janie's conversation with Pheoby makes clear, she has reflected on the choices Nanny and Joe made for her and concluded that respectability and material comfort are no substitutes for love and autonomy. Having survived marriage to Logan Killicks and Joe Starks, Janie concludes, "Dis ain't no business proposition, and no race after property and titles. Dis is uh love game" (114). Her rejection of respectable, conformist notions of love is confirmed when she accedes to Tea Cake's freewheeling ways with the money she brings to the marriage. Realizing sexual pleasure with Tea Cake, and enjoying his treatment of her as a person with desires of her own, Janie opens herself to love without reservations.

To read these chapters as the arrival of an ideal love requires reading in historical context. Most notable about the relationship, given the time period of the novel, is Tea Cake's insistence that Janie control her own money and his view that Janie is sturdy enough for the rough-and-tumble life he leads. In contemporary American society, women have many more options to support themselves aside from marriage; even conservative marriage paradigms acknowledge that women have their own ideas and opinions. Tea Cake's single-handed decision to take Janie's money without asking her would give any modern woman pause, and it gave Janie pause as well. His decision to determine their course—moving to the Everglades—would also be a sticking point for a more modern woman.

In this context, Hurston's full-throated celebration of sexual desire and romance as essential, valuable aspects of black women's identities was rare for the time period. Authors often represented African-American women as chaste and moral. They worked to disprove stereotypes of African-American women, as promiscuous Jezebels or asexual Mammy figures, that had dominated from the times of slavery. Many African-American characters sought to engage in racial uplift; in particular, African-American women heroines were respectable, conventional, middle-class figures who sacrificed everything for the race or their children. Janie, notably, makes no such sacrifices and has no children. She focuses on self-actualization.

Chapters 14-17

Chapter 14 Summary

Tea Cake knew how to navigate the seasonal work rhythm of the Everglades, so he insisted that the couple head down to Lake Okeechobee before the season began. His foresight allowed them to secure a worker's house, with plumbing, before the crowds of poor workers arrived. Before the season began, Tea Cake taught Janie to shoot; she had a knack for it, and hunted to put food on their table. Once the bean picking season began, Tea Cake worked in the fields all day and gambled most of the night while Janie kept house.

Eventually, Janie joined him in the fields after he told her he missed her too much during the day for her to continue to stay home. Janie's appearance in the fields convinced the other workers that she did not see herself as better than them, and the Woods household quickly became the center of social life out on the muck. For the first time, Janie participated in the verbal play and jokes, fully part of the community around her.

Chapter 15 Summary

Janie noticed that Nunkie, another woman who worked alongside them, flirted with Tea Cake, who did little to discourage Nunkie's interest. Things came to a head one day when Janie came across Nunkie and Tea Cake tussling on the ground away from the fields. Janie did not believe Tea Cake when he told her that he was attempting to get his work tickets from Nunkie, who stole them. Janie was not able to catch up with Nunkie because the woman ran away, so Janie headed home.

Janie and Tea Cake had a physical fight over Tea Cake's infidelity. He calmed her down by piling on top of her, and the two made love. Janie felt reassured the next morning when Tea Cake told her that he had no interest in Nunkie.

Chapter 16 Summary

Janie and Tea Cake decided to spend the off season on the muck. Mrs. Turner, a light-skinned, unattractive woman and restaurant owner, had internalized racist ideas about the superiority of white skin and the inferiority of African Americans. Her constant criticism of African Americans and black physical features irritated Tea Cake, but her efforts to get Janie to leave Tea Cake (who was dark skinned), and marry Mrs. Turner's light-skinned brother infuriated him. Tea Cake told Janie to snub Mrs. Turner, but Mrs. Turner idolized Janie's appearance—light skin and straight hair—so much that she accepted the snubs as her due.

Chapter 17 Summary

Tea Cake grew weary of Mrs. Turner's interference in his marriage, so he slapped Janie repeatedly, leaving visible bruises on her to show the Turners that he controlled the relationship. His coworkers in the fields admired his actions and felt envious that he had ownership over a woman light enough to show bruises.

Tea Cake finally got his revenge on Mrs. Turner by colluding with several friends to trash her restaurant during a brawl. Mrs. Turner decided to return to Miami. She found out later that her son and brother had already left after several of Tea Cake's friends threatened them.

Chapters 14-17 Analysis

Hurston was a keen observer of the colorism—internalized racism—in the African-American community. She uses Mrs. Turner to represent this form of self-hatred, and portrays Janie as a person who rejects the premises of colorism.

Mrs. Turner assumed herself superior, in every way, to her poorer and darker-skinned neighbors because of her light complexion and her ownership of a restaurant. To be black, in Mrs. Turner's imagination, was also to be poor. Her attempt to break up Tea Cake and Janie, so Janie could marry her brother, showed how Mrs. Turner policed race and class lines at the expense of her supposed morality. Mrs. Turner's hypocrisy becomes clear when other characters note her willingness to take money from the people she despises.

In the racialized hierarchy of a society that prized nothing that more closely approximated whiteness, Janie, a fair-skinned black woman with long, somewhat straight hair, was considered a prize. Janie rejected those values. She married Tea Cake, a man who had darker skin than she did. Janie also rejected classist assumptions that intersected with the internalized racism that existed in some parts of her community. She recognized and enjoyed participating in the storytelling rituals on the muck, fully part of the community in a way she'd never been at Eatonville. She repeatedly rejected Mrs. Turner's racist and classist pronouncements about her neighbors.

One of the more problematic episodes in the novel for modern readers is how Tea Cake resolved his sense of insecurity and anger over Mrs. Turner's colorism. He beat Janie to assert his masculinity and to send a message to the Turners. The affirmation he received illustrated that colorism was widespread, even among the black working class. Hurston chose not to represent Janie's reaction to this beating; in fact, Janie, the protagonist, is entirely absent in Chapter 17. This episode, likely intended to be humorous, shows that working-class African-American identity down on the muck is quite distinct from the "respectable," middle-class black identity advanced by many writers of the Harlem Renaissance.

Chapters 18-20

Chapter 18 Summary

Janie and Tea Cake were still down on the muck when the Seminoles and the Bahamians headed east despite the fact that the picking season was not complete. Both groups warned Janie and Tea Cake that a hurricane was coming; Tea Cake discounted their warnings, but even the animals began to flee.

Many of Tea Cake's friends gathered at his house to weather the storm, but when the winds came in, they grew fearful and realized staying behind had been a mistake. Tea Cake and Janie fled the house along with a friend when the winds grew stronger, and it became apparent that the dikes and dam works that held back the Okeechobee would break. They barely survived their flight to higher ground; the friend who accompanied them, Motorboat, stayed behind, too tired to keep running. During their flight, Tea Cake killed an aggressive dog that tried to attack Janie. The dog bit Tea Cake on the face. The couple reached Palm Beach, where they spent most of their money to secure a tiny sleeping space. They reaffirmed their love for each other.

Chapter 19 Summary

Tea Cake was forced to work burying bodies in Palm Beach when he was picked up as a vagrant (despite having money in his pocket). After he managed to escape, the couple returned to the Everglades, where things seemed to go well. Motorboat had napped through the remainder of the storm and survived, and Tea Cake quickly found work. After a month at home, Tea Cake fell ill and could not drink water. The doctor delivered bad news: Tea Cake likely had contracted rabies from the dog bite during the storm. Because treatment for rabies had to be given soon after the bite, Tea Cake would not survive.

The doctor told Janie to keep Tea Cake comfortable and to sleep separately from him in case he bit her during a fit of rage. Tea Cake grew increasingly paranoid, accusing Janie of cheating on him and even poisoning him. When he began to sleep with a loaded pistol under his pillow, Janie took precautions, including putting a rifle within reach. She still believed she could protect Tea Cake, despite signs that he was less and less himself and more and more his disease.

The worst finally happened: Tea Cake attempted to shoot Janie when he realized that Mrs. Turner's brother had returned to the muck; he believed that Janie planned to leave him. Janie killed Tea Cake to save her own life and was tried for murder by an all-white jury and judge. Although white women who came to gawk at the tragedy in the courtroom empathized with Janie, she felt wounded by African-American friends who willingly testified against her. Janie explained that she loved Tea Cake and only killed him in self-defense (Hurston does not directly represent this testimony). The jury found Janie not guilty.

Although Janie felt hurt by the reaction of Tea Cake's friends, she understood their love for Tea Cake drove their hostility toward her. She spared no expense on Tea Cake's funeral in West Palm Beach and invited all of his friends to see him off. She felt so grief stricken that she wore her old overalls to the funeral because she "was too busy feeling grief to dress like grief" (189), as she did when Joe Starks died.

Chapter 20 Summary

Janie has now finished her story. She tells Pheoby that she can tell all the town gossips any part of it because Janie no longer cares what they think. Janie says that people who don't have the ability to experience life spend all their time talking about people who do. People have to experience things for themselves, and those who have not are not worth listening to. Pheoby tells Janie she feels as if she "done growed 10 feet higher jus' listenin'" to Janie's story (192).

After Pheoby leaves, Janie goes up to her bedroom to think over her experiences and to mourn. As she reflects, she feels the spirit of Tea Cake come to her, and those memories are enough to make her feel like she is her own person. She no longer feels the need to venture down the

road or look to other people to find herself. She is enough
as she is.

Chapters 18-20 Analysis

Hurston packs a great deal into these last three chapters: the
storm, the trial, and Janie's return home. The novel's
conclusion wraps up the theme of African-American
women's identities and the centrality of storytelling in
Southern African-American culture. When Janie's story
ends, she has come into her own as a person. Hurston's
description of this moment—Janie "pull[ing] in her horizon
like a great fish net [...] from around the waist of the world
and drap[ing] it over her shoulder" (193)—makes the point
that because she has experienced enough of the world to
confidently proclaim her values, Janie now defines her own
sense of self. She does not need a man to come along down
the road to make sense of her experiences.

The ending brings Janie's development full circle by going
back to Nanny's hopes as an African-American woman.
Nanny's aim was to "to preach a great sermon about
colored women sittin' on high" (16), but she defined
"sittin' on high" as having material status, and she pushed
this dream on Janie. The "sermon" that Janie gives is a
story about love and freedom, one that liberates listeners,
particularly women and especially black women, from the
social pressure to define themselves by the men in their
lives. Hurston captures Pheoby's reaction as an analogue
for the reader; Janie' story enlarges both Pheoby's sense of
herself and her expectations about the possibilities of love.

Although the novel mostly ignores the white world around
the edges of Eatonville, the latter chapters show both racist
and sexist limits imposed on African-American women of
the time. The all-white jury in the courtroom during Janie's

trial had the power of life and death over Janie as she pled for them to understand why she killed Tea Cake in self-defense. Although the resentment from Tea Cake's friends was mostly poorly expressed grief, they presciently observed that Tea Cake's gender and dark skin, as well as Janie's appearance—more closely approximating whiteness—played a role in Janie's acquittal. Janie and Tea Cake's conversation about needing whites to vouch for African Americans shows how Jim Crow laws and white supremacy curtailed the mobility and freedom of African Americans.

CHARACTER ANALYSIS

Janie Crawford

The protagonist of the novel, Janie Crawford, is a light-skinned, long-haired African-American woman—the product of two generations of rape—who begins the novel as an object of curiosity and past scandal. To her friend Pheoby, she recounts her life story and the quest for love that led to the scandal.

Janie's ideas of love and sexuality began when she was an idealistic 16-year-old with a strong desire for physical and emotional connection, as seen in her coming-of-age moment beneath the pear tree. Janie's grandmother, however, saw marriage as an arrangement designed to ensure security. Nanny pushed her to marry Logan Killicks, a crude but financially secure farmer that Janie did not love. The marriage failed when she left Logan and married Joe Starks, a self-important man who convinced her that marrying him would fulfill her desire for adventure. She moved to Eatonville to help him build the new town, but Joe had very traditional notions of marriage and women. She spent the decades between her teens and her 40s unsatisfied, living in obedience and silence, conforming to Joe's expectations.

Janie finally achieved some degree of freedom after Joe's death. She followed her heart by marrying Vergible "Tea Cake" Woods, whose lack of wealth and young age scandalized Eatonville. She took up life as a seasonal migrant, and the autonomy and wide experience she had during these two years satisfied her desire for freedom and movement; the intense relationship with Tea Cake satisfied her emotionally. Their love ended tragically, but it gave Janie full control of her own life and identity. Janie ends the story as a character in command of who she is, no longer caring what the people of Eatonville think of her.

Nanny Crawford

Born a slave, Nanny Crawford was Janie's grandmother. She bore her master's child and reared her granddaughter after that child, at 17, lost her mind following the sexual assault that impregnated her with Janie. Nanny's ideas about love, sex, and respectability grew out of both her experience as an enslaved woman and out of watching her daughter be exploited. She believed African-American women should marry for material security and that love and physical desire should be negligible considerations. She forced Janie to marry Logan Killicks but died shortly after, when she realized that her dreams for Janie were perhaps wrong-headed.

Joe Starks

Joe "Jody" Starks was Janie's second husband. An ambitious man, he convinced Janie to move to Eatonville, where he eventually became the mayor. Joe changed little over the course of their marriage: He remained self-important and thrived on bending others to his will. He resorted to taunts and physical abuse when his self-image was threatened, expected Janie to obey him unquestioningly, and built Eatonville as a monument to himself. He forced Janie to assume the identity of the dutiful, middle-class wife, never delivering the passion she imagined beneath the pear tree. He died of kidney failure.

Vergible " Tea Cake" Woods

Tea Cake was Janie's third husband, a handsome, dark-skinned gambler and adventurer who wooed Janie by treating her as a woman with desires of her own. Also a bluesman who played guitar and piano, he represented the fulfillment of Janie's desires, and their love allowed Janie to have experiences she only dreamed about for much of her life.

Pheoby Watson

Pheoby is Janie's best friend in the town of Eatonville, entrenched in the community but a fierce defender and loyal companion. Pheoby listens to Janie's story and by the end, considers herself transformed and no longer satisfied with her own life.

Leafy

Leafy Crawford was Janie's mother, the product of a forced relationship between Nanny and her master; she had light skin, hair, and eyes, which she passed onto her daughter. Raised to fulfill Nanny's dreams of respectability, Leafy lost her mind after a brutal assault by a teacher. Unable to recover psychologically after the rape, which caused her to conceive and give birth to Janie, Leafy wandered and lived in the forest.

Mrs. Turner

Mrs. Turner was a light-skinned woman who owned a restaurant in the community where Janie lived with Tea Cake. Mrs. Turner was proud of her light skin and believed it made her better than darker-skinned people like Tea Cake. After Mrs. Turner attempted to break up Janie and Tea Cake so Janie could marry Mrs. Turner's brother, Tea Cake and his friends conspired to run her and her family out of town. Mrs. Turner's beliefs about white superiority were a prime example of colorism, a form of internalized racism.

The Long Harlem Renaissance

Zora Neale Hurston published *Their Eyes Were Watching God* in 1937 during the Great Depression and long after the 1920s height of the Harlem Renaissance, an artistic and cultural movement during which African Americans asserted their right to self-representation. Nevertheless, Hurston's novel is an important work that both shows the influence of the movement on African-American literature and expands its umbrella to cover not only African Americans living in the Northeast and Mid-Atlantic but also Southern African Americans, who had a unique and vibrant culture of their own.

During the Harlem Renaissance, writers and artists sought to celebrate the beauty, creativity, and originality of African-American culture. Writers such as W.E.B. DuBois and Alain Locke saw these artistic contributions as proof that African Americans were full citizens during an age when Jim Crow laws and mob violence prevented the full exercise of their rights. Artists and critics who embraced the political program of the Harlem Renaissance felt pressure to present positive images to white audiences in an effort to rehabilitate the image of African Americans. The old but still dominant image of African Americans in the minds of many Americans was that African Americans were rural, Southern people, uneducated and stuck in the past. African-American women were either the sexless mammies of slavery time or promiscuous Jezebels who tempted virtuous white men into sin.

As an antidote to such negative images, writers presented African Americans as a people who participated in modernity and fully committed to fighting racism. Earlier writers highlighted respectable, virtuous, middle-class characters to counter negative images of African Americans. Younger writers like Langston Hughes presented African Americans as the sophisticated and modern people who created jazz and used slang that marked them as city dwellers. That this "New Negro" was most frequently a man reflects the gender inequality of the time. In much work of the early Harlem Renaissance, African-American women are portrayed as absent, as objects who do not speak for themselves, or as one-dimensional domestic goddesses who give up everything for others or racial uplift.

Hurston pushed back against the pressure to represent African Americans in this mold. Although she did write short fiction set in the city, *Their Eyes Were Watching God* is set in the rural South and legitimizes the culture of Southern African Americans. Although the characters speak in dialect, and certain set pieces would not be out of place on the minstrel stage, Hurston's female protagonist ultimately refuses to sacrifice herself for the men in her life or for the middle-class respectability so central to novels of the day.

Hurston's novel is a bookend to the Harlem Renaissance. Her novel went out of print for decades but was rediscovered by Alice Walker and other African-American women during the 1960s, as an important forerunner for black feminism.

African-American Women and Identity

Their Eyes Were Watching God, a *bildungsroman* that follows Janie's development from teen to mature woman, raises significant issues related to the representation of African-American women. Janie increasingly rejects the racial and gender norms of her community, chooses love over material prosperity, and seizes a freedom rarely achieved by any woman of the day, regardless of her race.

Her first marriage to Logan Killicks, a crude but relatively prosperous man, fulfills Nanny's expectation that her secure her future by marrying property owner. For a woman who has owned little—not even herself at one point since she came of age during slavery—the idea of property as security was irresistible.

Nanny's experiences as the concubine of her slave master, the object of jealousy by her slave mistress, and the mother of a daughter whose mind is broken by rape reinforced her sense that love and desire were threats best neutralized by conventional morality. In including Nanny's story, Hurston demonstrates the lasting and damaging impact of sexual exploitation on African-American women, even after the arrival of freedom. Despite having escaped slavery, Nanny never feels secure enough in her own person to pass down the vision of love and the free play of sexual desire that Janie eventually embraces.

Hurston captures Janie's early notion of love and sexual desire in the scene of the pear tree at the start of the novel, using nature imagery to present women's desires as essential aspects of identity that should not be hidden away or considered shameful. Janie tried to make her vision under the pear tree real, despite pressure from her husbands, neighbors, and Nanny's voice in her head to be content with a much more conventional life.

Janie married Joe Starks, seduced in part by his expansive vision of what an African American could be and by his grand plans for Eatonville. As "Mrs. Mayor Starks" (110), Janie conformed to the expectation of the townspeople, who saw her as an embodiment of their material aspirations and nothing else. She also accepted the dominance of her husband, who saw her as one possession—among many—that elevated him above his peers. Janie spent decades burying her voice in order to fulfill this image of middle-class respectability. Near the end of Joe's life, Janie's voice erupted in the store after one too many of Joe's public humiliations. After Joe's death, Janie secured the material means to be financially independent, outlasting Joe by maintaining her silence and tamping down her own sexuality long enough to become a rich widow.

With no children, a circumstance that freed her from the requirement that she sacrifice her life and dreams for her offspring, Janie at last began to engage in increasingly overt self-expression. She courted and married a man who was poor with darker skin, but who satisfied her sexually and fed her desire for adventure. When she went to Jacksonville and the muck with Tea Cake, she escaped the rigid domestic space that had confined her for much of her life.

Although Hurston presents the relationship with Tea Cake as something very close to a fairytale romance, the relationship is not without flaws. Hurston carefully shows how Janie's movements are still tied to that of her husband, how conflicts are caused by gender expectations on both sides, and how Janie's fate—especially during the hurricane in the Everglades—is determined by Tea Cake's decisions. Janie followed Tea Cake out of love, bucking societal expectations, a shift from her previous marriages.

The ending of the novel and the frame narrative—Janie telling a story to her friend, Pheoby Watson—show the power of a woman coming into her own. Janie's story does not end in marriage for the sake of marriage, or self-sacrifice to uplift the race. Janie is alone but claims an identity without reference to men. In the end, Janie becomes a storyteller who has earned her rightful place on the porch. In the courtroom, her telling of the story of her love of Tea Cake and the tragedy of his death is so powerful that it overcomes institutional racism and the disapproval of her own community. Pheoby's reaction to Janie's story—that listening to it has made her "10 feet higher" (192)—shows that Janie's voice has expanded Pheoby's own notions of what it means to be an African-American woman.

African-American Folk Culture and Language

Hurston, a native of Eatonville and a Columbia University-trained anthropologist, with fieldwork in the Deep South and Haiti to her credit, unapologetically pushed against the trend of representing all African Americans as city dwellers and sophisticates at home in modern culture. In *Their Eyes Were Watching God*, she makes rural, Southern, African-American culture the most significant cultural context for the work, using dialect and language that celebrates the richness of African-American folk life.

There are three distinct forms of language in the novel: direct discourse, usually in the form of dialect; the voice of the narrator, a direct presentation to the reader in standard American English; and free indirect discourse, when the voices of the narrator and Janie blend—this discourse is generally in standard American English but includes idioms and imagery associated with African-American folk culture. Hurston bridges the perceived gap between literary language and the vivid but frequently disrespected language of African-American folk culture. Her inclusion of the outrageous stories of the porch-sitters in Eatonville makes a strong argument that, far from being characterized by backwardness, this culture and its language should be celebrated and documented.

The use of standard American English by the narrator, especially for exposition and commentary, makes the connection between this culturally specific story and universal themes. The opening lines of the novel, for example, show that although this is a story about African Americans, it is also one about the distinct experiences of men and women.

Finally, the use of free indirect discourse shows that African American folk idioms and imagery drawn from the rural South have a home in American literature. Hurston's free indirect discourse welcomes the reader into the world of these characters using language that straddles the world of the reader and of her characters.

The Pear Tree

Hurston uses the pear tree and its bees, pollen, flowers, and honey as symbols of sex and desire throughout the novel. Hurston introduces the central image with the literal pear tree that Janie observes one afternoon when she is 16. Her rapturous observation of the process of pollination—the means by which life is propagated for plants—reflects Janie's sexual awakening and the desires that her grandmother deems acceptable. The pear tree also normalizes women's sexual desire during a time when such expressions were still seen as taboo.

Hurston has Janie express her disappointment in the lack of a sexual charge with Logan as "desecrating the pear tree" (14), meaning that he does not fulfill her vision of the ideal lover. This same sense of disappointment is apparent when Janie begins to know Joe more intimately. She recognizes from the first that he does not "represent sun-up and pollen and blooming trees" (29), but his vision still attracts her. When Janie finally does encounter her ideal, Tea Cake, she describes him as "bee to a blossom—a pear tree blossom in the spring" (106). They are sexually compatible.

Janie's Hair

Janie's hair is long and somewhat straight; it symbolizes her sexuality and her femininity. It is also an important marker of the impact of colorism on black beauty standards.

Without exception, Janie's hair is the first thing her three husbands remark upon as one of the reasons why they find her attractive. Joe Stark's impulse once he marries Janie is to force her to cover her hair in public and thus assert his control over her sexuality. One of Janie's first acts after his death is to burn the scarves he forced her to wear and thus reclaim control over her own body and desires. Tea Cake seems to find her hair irresistible, so when Janie accepts his crossing of personal boundaries by grooming her hair while she sleeps, Janie is indicating that she will accept his love. Her long plait, when she returns to the town after the death of Tea Cake, is just one of many indications that she is still sexually potent even though she is in middle age at that point.

The emphasis on the length and texture of Janie's hair is a topic of frequent conversation throughout the novel. The fetishization of her hair partly reflects the fact that long, uncoiled hair more closely approximates the hair of prosperous white women. As the conflict between Tea Cake and the Turners makes clear, colorism—the internalized racism of African Americans who celebrate closer proximity to whites—is an important reason for the perception that Janie is beautiful.

The Road and the Horizon

From the very beginning of the novel, Hurston uses the road and the horizon to symbolize Janie's hunger for experience and freedom. At the start of the novel, Janie waits at the road for someone or something to happen to her. Her passivity and inability to see what is over the horizon show her acceptance of societal norms, which dictate that women's lives and experiences must be shaped by others. Once Janie steps out onto the road with Tea Cake, however, she assumes more control over her life and embraces a wider experience, even though she still follows after a man to determine the course of her life.

At the end of the novel, Janie clears "road-dust out of her hair" (192) and "pull[s] the horizon" in and "drape[s] it over her shoulder" (193), metaphorical acts that symbolize her newfound self-sufficiency. She no longer needs the road or the horizon to understand who she is.

The Muck

The muck is the Everglades of Florida, an important symbol of the diversity of the South and of Janie's deep engagement with life once she sets out on the road with Tea Cake. In the muck, Janie encounters Seminoles and Bahamians who congregate on the muck seasonally to work in the fields. This mix of cultures is an accurate reflection of the other South, one that includes more than African Americans and whites.

Being in the muck is literally about getting muddied up. For Janie, who has spent her life from 16 through her 40s trapped in a store and in her second husband's big house, living in the muck puts her in close contact with working-class people. Her engagement with her neighbors on the muck is her first opportunity to participate fully in the life and culture of the South, making the muck an important precondition for her achievement of self at this stage in the novel.

The Mule

The mule is a literal and metaphorical figure in the novel associated with labor and burdens. Nanny tells Janie, "De nigger woman is de mule uh de world so fur as Ah can see. Ah been prayin' fah it tuh be different" (14). Nanny uses the mule to speak to her experience as an enslaved woman who is forced to have her master's children and to labor in other ways that ignore her desire for self-expression and freedom. Hurston uses the mule to express the multiple forms of oppression African-American women face as a result of race, gender, and class.

There is also a literal mule in the story, the one who belongs to Matt Bonner and around whom a whole mythology springs up in Eatonville. The ways the community interacts with the mule—Joe buying the mule to put him out to pasture and the mule's funeral—shows the importance of folk and storytelling culture in the novel.

The Porch

Hurston uses the porch of the store in Eatonville as a symbol of community and of the centrality of storytelling to African Americans in the South. The porch dwellers serve as a chorus that articulates the values of the community as they both look down on and envy Janie's violation of those values. The porch is also the scene of courtships, conflicts, and verbal contests that establish the social hierarchy in the town.

Logan Killicks's Land

Logan Killicks is the owner of 60 acres—20 more acres than the 40 acres that African Americans believed would be the foundation of financial security after their emancipation from slavery. His 60 acres represent black material prosperity, while the misery that exists between Logan and Janie, despite these 60 acres, shows that material prosperity will never be a replacement for happiness.

The Courtroom

Janie is forced to fight for her life by testifying on her own behalf in a courtroom presided over by a white judge and a white jury. The courtroom is also a site where whites explicitly silence Tea Cake's friends by reminding them that their race prevents them from having any standing. The court is one of the novel's few overt symbols of white supremacy and power over the lives of African Americans.

The Hurricane

Their Eyes Were Watching God draws most of its metaphors and imagery from nature, and the most potent symbol of the role of nature in the lives of the characters is the hurricane that lands in the Everglades. Setting into motion the chain of events that ends with Tea Cake's death, the hurricane represents the capriciousness not only of nature but also of God, who fails to answer the prayers of many whose "eyes were watching God" for signs that they might survive the storm (160). The hurricane highlights that in the universe Hurston creates, survival turns out to be a question of chance and choices rather than fate.

IMPORTANT QUOTES

1. "Ships at a distance have every man's wish on board. For some they come in with the tide. For others they sail forever on the horizon, never out of sight, never landing until the Watcher turns his eyes away in resignation, his dreams mocked to death by Time. That is the life of men. Now, women forget all those things they don't want to remember, and remember everything they don't want to forget. The dream is the truth. Then they act and do things accordingly." (Chapter 1, Page 1)

   Hurston's opening lines introduce both the importance of differences between men and women's experiences, and the horizon, which symbolizes the possibilities that are excluded and implied by the one's identity. A "Watcher," Janie transitions from passively waiting for life to happen to becoming a woman who acts. This quote previews of the arc of her character and the plot.

2. "It was the time for sitting on porches beside the road. It was the time to hear things and talk. These sitters had been tongueless, earless, eyeless conveniences all day long. Mules and other brutes had occupied their skins. But now, the sun and the bossman were gone, so the skins felt power and human. They became lords of sounds and lesser things. They passed nations through their mouths. They sat in judgment." (Chapter 1, Page 1)

   Hurston introduces the porch, the gathering place for the town of Eatonville. The power and ability of the porch-sitters to pass judgment shows the centrality of the storytelling culture to the identity of the people who sit there—mostly working-class people who expend much of their energy just surviving.

3. "Ah don't mean to bother wid tellin' 'em nothin',
   Pheoby. 'Tain't worth de trouble. You can tell 'em
   what Ah say if you wants to. Dat's just de same as me
   'cause mah tongue is in mah friend's mouf." (Chapter
   1, Page 6)

   *Janie's trust shows the importance of Pheoby's
   friendship. Janie's statement also shows her willingness
   to violate community norms no matter what: She is a
   free woman.*

4. "She was stretched on her back beneath the pear tree
   soaking in the alto chant of the visiting bees, the gold of
   the sun and the panting breath of the breeze when the
   inaudible voice of it all came to her. She saw a dust-
   bearing bee sink into the sanctum of a bloom; the
   thousand sister-calyxes arch to meet the love embrace
   and the ecstatic shiver of the tree from root to tiniest
   branch creaming in every blossom and frothing with
   delight. So this was a marriage!" (Chapter 2, Page 11)

   *The pear tree, which Janie first saw as a 16-year-old
   girl, symbolizes Janie's burgeoning awareness of her
   sexual identity. She repeatedly turned to the pear tree
   as a vision of idealized love and desire.*

5. "De nigger woman is de mule uh de world so fur as Ah
   can see. Ah been prayin' fah it tuh be different wid you.
   Lawd, Lawd, Lawd!" (Chapter 2, Page 14)

   *Nanny articulated the triple burden of poverty, racism,
   and sexism that African-American women face in an
   unfair world.*

6. "Ah didn't want to be used for a work-ox and a brood-
   sow and Ah didn't want mah daughter used dat way

neither. It sho wasn't mah will for things to happen lak they did. Ah even hated de way you was born. But, all de same Ah said thank God, Ah got another chance. Ah wanted to preach a great sermon about colored women sittin' on high, but they wasn't no pulpit for me. Freedom found me wid a baby daughter in mah arms, so Ah said Ah'd take a broom and a cook-pot and throw up a highway through de wilderness for her. She would expound what Ah felt. But somehow she got lost offe de highway and next thing Ah knowed here you was in de world. So whilst Ah was tendin' you of nights Ah said Ah'd save de text for you." (Chapter 2, Page 16)

Nanny's description of herself emphasized the exploitation under which she labored as an enslaved woman, while her description of Leafy's fate showed how trauma narrowed her vision of what was possible for her granddaughter. Janie struggled against Nanny's belief in the virtue of owning things for much of her life.

7. "She knew that God tore down the old world every evening and built a new one by sun-up. It was wonderful to see it take form with the sun and emerge from the gray dust of its making. The familiar people and things had failed her so she hung over the gate and looked up the road towards way off. She knew now that marriage did not make love. Janie's first dream was dead, so she became a woman." (Chapter 3, Page 25)

Janie's vision of marriage as romantic love rapidly eroded as a result of the decidedly unromantic relationship she had with Logan. Recognizing that this vision was an ideal and not reality showed that Janie had come of age.

8. "Every day after that they managed to meet in the scrub oaks across de road and talk about when he would be a big ruler of things with her reaping the benefits. Janie pulled back a long time because he did not represent sun-up and pollen and blooming trees, but he spoke for far horizon. He spoke for change and chance. Still she hung back. The memory of Nanny was still powerful and strong." (Chapter 4, Page 29)

Janie loss of her idealized vision of love led her to accept Joe Starks as a partner because he fed another vision she had for herself: as a person who could experience a life beyond the confines of rural, racist Florida. Her initial hesitation turned out to be wise; although he had ambitions for himself, those plans would not allow Janie to have autonomy.

9. "He was very solemn and helped her to the seat beside him. With him on it, it sat like some high, ruling chair. From now on until death she was going to have flower dust and springtime sprinkled over everything. A bee for her bloom. Her old thoughts were going to come in handy now, but new words would have to be made and said to fit them." (Chapter 4, Page 32)

The reference to the "high, ruling chair" shows how Janie unwittingly stepped onto a pedestal that limited her freedom as a woman (32). Janie's misconception that life with Joe would meet her idealized notion was also indicated by her assumption that he would be "the bee for her bloom" (32), the vision of love she had under the pear tree

10. "Janie made her face laugh after a short pause, but it wasn't too easy. She had never thought of making a speech, and didn't know if she cared to make one at all.

It must have been the way Joe spoke out without giving her a chance to say anything one way or another that took the bloom off of things. But anyway, she went down the road behind him that night feeling cold. He strode along invested with his new dignity, thought and planned out loud, unconscious of her thoughts." (Chapter 5, Page 43)

Janie finally realized that marriage to Joe would require her to relinquish her self-expression. Joe's cluelessness revealed that he embraced traditional notions of womanhood.

11. "She stood there until something fell off the shelf inside her. Then she went inside there to see what it was. It was her image of Jody tumbled down and shattered. But looking at it she saw that it never was the flesh and blood figure of her dreams, just something she had grabbed up to drape her dreams over. In a way she turned her back upon the image where it lay and looked further. She had no more blossomy openings dusting pollen over her man, neither any glistening young fruit where the petals used to be [...] She was saving up feelings for some man she had never seen. She had an inside and an outside now and suddenly she knew how not to mix them." (Chapter 6, Page 72)

After Joe slapped her over a poorly cooked meal, Janie realized that she'd been immature to believe he would fulfill her ideals. The reference to having an inside and outside shows how she learned to conform to gendered expectations, at least outwardly, in order to survive.

12. "'Naw, Ah ain't no young gal no mo' but den Ah ain't no old woman neither. Ah reckon Ah looks mah age too. But Ah'm uh woman every inch of me, and Ah

know it. Dat's uh whole lot more'n you kin say. You big-bellies round here and put out a lot of brag, but 'tain't nothin' to it but yo' big voice. Humph! Talkin' 'bout me lookin' old! When you pull down yo' britches, you look lak de change uh life.'" (Chapter 7, Page 79)

As she entered her 40s, Janie finally wearied of Joe's public humiliation and decided to respond in harsh terms in a public setting—the store—when he attacked her. Her public retaliation signaled her unwillingness to conform to gendered expectations that she would be a meek and quiet wife.

13. "Janie starched and ironed her face and came set in the funeral behind her veil. It was like a wall of stone and steel. The funeral was going on outside. All things concerning death and burial were said and done. Finish. End. Nevermore. Darkness. Deep hole. Dissolution. Eternity. Weeping and wailing outside. Inside the expensive black folds were resurrection and life. She did not reach outside for anything, nor did the things of death reach inside to disturb her calm. She sent her face to Joe's funeral, and herself went rollicking with the springtime across the world." (Chapter 9, Page 88)

The difference between Janie's subjective state of celebration and her exterior mourning showed her recognition that Joe's death granted her freedom. She kept these emotions to herself because she recognized that joy would violate societal norms for grieving women.

14. "Here Nanny had taken the biggest thing God ever made, the horizon—for no matter how far a person can go die horizon is still way beyond you—and pinched it in to such a little bit of a thing that she could tie it about

her granddaughter's neck tight enough to choke her. She hated the old woman who had twisted her so in the name of love." (Chapter 9, Page 89)

Janie finally realized the negative impact of Nanny's notions of security and love. In rejecting Nanny, Janie embraced an identity not shaped by the trauma of slavery, and turned her back on Nanny's materialism.

15. "He looked like the love thoughts of women. He could be a bee to a blossom—a pear tree blossom in the spring. He seemed to be crushing scent out of the world with his footsteps. Crushing aromatic herbs with every step he took. Spices hung about him. He was a glance from God." (Chapter 11, Page 106)

Janie's first impression of Tea Cake, which included the natural imagery and the pear tree references, made it clear that Tea Cake met her idealized vision of masculinity.

16. "'If people thinks de same they can make it all right, so in the beginning new thoughts had tuh be thought and new words said. After Ah got used tuh dat, we gits 'long jus' fine. He done taught me de maiden language all over.'" (Chapter 12, Page 115)

Janie was willing to violate gendered norms to be with Tea Cake because he helped her experience life in a way no other man had before. The relationship with Tea Cake was thus a crucial part of Janie's development as a woman.

17. "He drifted off into sleep and Janie looked down on him and felt a self-crushing love. So her soul crawled out from its hiding place." (Chapter 13, Page 128)

Despite Tea Cake's actions—gambling and taking her money without permission—Janie decided to trust him. Her willingness to be vulnerable to him contrasted with the way she hid who she really was from Joe.

18. "Mrs. Turner, like all other believers had built an altar to the unattainable—Caucasian characteristics for all. Her god would smite her, would hurl her from pinnacles and lose her in deserts, but she would not forsake his altars. Behind her crude words was a belief that somehow she and others through worship could attain her paradise—a heaven of straight-haired, thin-lipped, high-nose boned white seraphs." (Chapter 16, Page 145)

Hurston describes the hypocrisy and self-hatred involved in colorism practiced by people like Mrs. Turner.

19. "They sat in company with the others in other shanties, their eyes straining against crude walls and their souls asking if He meant to measure their puny might against His. They seemed to be staring at the dark, but their eyes were watching God." (Chapter 18, Page 160)

Janie and the community on the muck confront nature as an overwhelming force, a symbol of the unknowability of God. The title of the novel speaks to the burdens of life as an African American in the South, struggling against exploitation and poverty, always on the lookout for God's perceived tests and judgments, and His mercy.

20. "It was the meanest moment of eternity. A minute before she was just a scared human being fighting for its life. Now she was her sacrificing self with Tea

Cake's head in her lap. She had wanted him to live so much and he was dead. No hour is ever eternity, but it has its right to weep." (Chapter 19, Page 184)

Janie felt conflicted the moment after she had to defend herself by killing Tea Cake. The moment was deeply tragic, but also one in which Janie, perhaps for the first time, chose herself over others.

21. "The court set and Janie saw the judge who had put on a great robe to listen about her and Tea Cake. And 12 more white men had stopped whatever they were doing to listen and pass on what happened between Janie and Tea Cake Woods, and as to whether things were done right or not. That was funny too. Twelve strange men who didn't know a thing about people like Tea Cake and her were going to sit on the thing. Eight or 10 white women had come to look at her too. They wore good clothes and had the pinky color that comes of good food. They were nobody's poor white folks. What need had they to leave their richness to come look on Janie in her overalls?" (Chapter 19, Page 185)

This scene in the courtroom was one of the few in which whites explicitly played a role in the lives of the African Americans. Janie's bemusement over their curiosity made it clear that their perspectives were not particularly important to her, despite their power. Janie's irreverent attitude captured Hurston's implicit belief that there was no need to plead for white respect for African-American culture.

22. "It was not death she feared. It was misunderstanding. If they made a verdict that she didn't want Tea Cake and wanted him dead, then that was a real sin and a shame." (Chapter 19, Page 188)

Janie's worried that the court, lacking the important cultural and personal contexts of her life, would misunderstand her testimony. This concern highlighted Janie's understanding of the court proceedings as part of a story over which she wished to exercise control, despite her lack of systemic power as an African-American woman.

23. "Lawd! […] Ah done growed 10 feet higher from jus' listenin' tuh you, Janie. Ah ain't satisfied wid mahself no mo.' Ah means tuh make Sam take me fishin' wid him after this. Nobody better not criticize yuh in mah hearin." (Chapter 20, Page 192)

Pheoby's reaction shows the power of Janie's story to expand the range of identities available to African-American women.

24. "Now, Pheoby, don't feel too mean wid de rest of 'em 'cause dey's parched up from not knowin' things. Dem meatskins is *got* tuh rattle tuh make out they's alive. Let 'em consolate theyselves wid talk. 'Course, talkin' don't amount tuh uh hill uh beans when yuh can't do nothin' else. And listenin' tuh dat kind uh talk is jus' lak openin' yo' mouth and lettin' de moon shine down yo' throat. It's uh known fact, Pheoby, you got tuh *go* there tuh *know* there. Yo' papa and yo' mama and nobody else can't tell yuh and show yuh. Two things everybody's got tuh do fuh theyselves. They got tuh go tuh God, and they got tub find out about livin' fuh theyselves." (Chapter 20, Page 192)

Janie shares her hard-earned wisdom, gained through years of conforming to other people's ideas about how to conduct her life as a woman, to make the argument that personal experience is the best teacher.

25. "She pulled in her horizon like a great fish-net. Pulled it from around the waist of the world and draped it over her shoulder. So much of life in its meshes! She called in her soul to come and see." (Chapter 20, Page 193)

Having experienced life on her own terms and rejected Nanny's limited horizons, Janie claims an identity in her own right, one that is not dependent on external exploration or relationships with men. She feels complete on her own.

ESSAY TOPICS

1. Janie has three significant relationships with men over the course of the novel. How does each relationship shape her understanding of herself? How is the quest for the love she envisioned beneath the pear tree intertwined with how she sees herself as a woman?

2. Hurston uses several different types of discourse in the novel. Describe the types of language she uses, and discuss the impact of that language on the representation of characters and African-American culture.

3. Hurston's novel briefly went out of print, but it was rediscovered during the 1960s by African-American women doing early black feminist work. Research this rediscovery. What about the novel captured the attention of writers such as Alice Walker?

4. Discuss the impact of slavery on African-American women's identity in the novel.

5. Discuss how the novel both extends and counters prevailing trends of the Harlem Renaissance.

6. Discuss how the novel's historical and cultural setting impacts its characters.

7. Discuss Hurston's use of natural imagery in the novel.

8. What does Janie mean when she says, "you got tuh *go* there tuh *know* there" (192), and how does Hurston use the plot of the novel to illustrate this belief?

9. Discuss the centrality of storytelling to the community and characters Hurston represents in the novel.

10. Hurston primarily focuses on a setting and characters that are African American. What impact does this choice have on the representation of African-American culture? When whites do appear in the novel, how does Hurston represent them, and what point does she seem to be making with these episodes?